MORE
BLACK
MEMORABILIA

A Handbook & Pri

Jan Lindenberger

77 Lower Valley Road, Atglen, PA 19310

Bakelite porter pin. "England." 4.5".
$150-175.

Copyright © 1995 by Jan Lindenberger.
Library of Congress Cataloging-in-Publication Data
Lindenberger, Jan.
    More black memorabilia/Jan Lindenberger.
        p. cm.
    Includes bibliographical references (p.) and index.
    ISBN 0-88740-733-1 (soft)
    1. Afro-Americans--Collectibles--Catalogs. I. Title.
NK839.3.A35L56 1995
973'.0496073'0075--dc20   94-37616
                                           CIP

Printed in Hong Kong.
ISBN: 0-88740-733-1

Published by Schiffer Publishing, Ltd.
77 Lower Valley Road
Atglen, PA 19310
Please write for a free catalog.
This book may be purchased from the publisher.
Please include $2.95 postage.
Try your bookstore first.

We are interested in hearing from authors
with book ideas on related subjects.

Title Page Photo:
Pottery natives salt and pepper set with
white man in boiling pot as a jelly
container. 5.5" natives; 5" jelly jar. Japan.
$125-150.

Acknowledgments

A special thank you to the following people for allowing me to photograph in their shops and from their collections, and also to anyone whom I may have missed.

The Antique Gallery, Colorado Springs, Colorado
Hampden Street Antique Market, Denver, Colorado
Colorado Antique Gallery, Littleton, Colorado
Sunday Traveler Antiques, Brazil, Indiana
Park City Mall, Park City, Kansas
Annie's Antique Mall, Park City, Kansas
Swap Shop Antique Mall, Severy, Kansas
Antique Plaza of Topeka, Topeka, Kansas
A Little of Everything, Wichita, Kansas
Holts Country Store, Grandview, Missouri
Main Street Mall, Ozark, Missouri
I-29 Antique Mall, Platte City, Missouri
Dime Store Days Mall, Fremont, Nebraska
Q Street Mall, Lincoln, Nebraska
I Remember Antiques, Omaha, Nebraska
Wanda Synhorst, Waterloo, Nebraska
Venice Antiques, Waterloo, Nebraska
Rose Fontanella, Brooklyn, New York
Route 66 Antique Mall, El Reno, Oklahoma
Unique Memories, Bradford, Pennsylvania
Antique Attractions, Erie, Pennsylvania
Jalosky's, Franklin, Pennsylvania
What Not Shop, Girard, Pennsylvania
Barbs Collectibles, Rillton, Pennsylvania

Cast iron paperweight turtle. Has pin back on top. 1900. "Maryland labor agency. We furnish labors white or colored." Rare. $350-400.

Preface

Black items were being produced as early as the 1700s. These included black dolls and fine porcelain figurines produced in Japan, Germany, France, England, Austria, and the United States. From the late 1800s, souvenirs were the biggest market for black memorabilia, such as figurines, salt and pepper sets, and bisque boys sitting on cotton bales. At the same time several useful items for the home came into play. Hot pads, pot holders, table cloths, spoon rests, clocks salt and pepper sets were among the many practical things on which black images appeared. Most of the items displayed a large mammy or chef working in the kitchen, a butler with a serving tray, or children with watermelons or chickens.

In the late 1950s and early 1960s the stereotyped obese, servant-look disappeared, and black collectibles were no longer being mass produced. Through the 1970s the few things that did stay in production did not have the grotesque look of their predecessors.

Grotesque figures are still in the antique market, but it seems the African-American collectors are the people searching them out. Why would they collect items that are stereotypical and derogatory? The reason seems to be that African-Americans want to show their children how other races have viewed them, and how times and attitudes have changed. Malinda Saunders, a black show promoter from Washington, D.C., confirmed that most of the approximately 30,000 collectors they themselves are black. They collect to preserve their history and to educate their children how it used to be and how the white person perceived them.

Boy and girl cotton-stuffed dolls over stocking material. 1930s. 5". $95-120 pair.

Contents

Majolica cigarette and match holder.
Austria. 5". $525-550.

Ceramic mammy string holder. String comes out the belly. Japan. $165-185.

Introduction

Black memorabilia is still one of the hottest items being collected today, although it is growing harder and harder to find to find good pieces. I remember when, only a few years ago, I would find a piece in almost every shop I went into. Today, I travel miles before I can find anything worthwhile.

The most collected items are the kitchen items. Wall pockets, mammy memos, salt and peppers, cookie jars, etc. The smiling mammies are my personal favorite. Slave documents, shackles, newspaper articles, photographs and other historical items are rising in popularity among collectors. There is a black history museum in Omaha, Nebraska that one can get an education about the historical aspect of these memorabilia.

It takes a special person to collect the finer pieces. Majolica items, porcelain figurines, and mechanical toys are very pricey and extremely rare. Most of the quality items are in private or personal collections, although one does surface occasionally The piece on the bottom of page 159, is in my collection and came from the Pennsylvania area. It's a tobacco leaf with a young man emerging out of the center of the leaf. One would go a long way to find another such wonderful piece, so this one will stay in my collection.

Ceramic Rio Rita candle stick holders by "Fritz and Floyd." 6". $75-90.

Most of the black memorabilia sold today was made and sold as souvenirs to the traveler. Salt and pepper sets had "souvenir of New Orleans" or other towns stamped on them, and were sold as a reminder of a trip in these location. They, of course, were made in Japan. Figurines and so-called "comical" items, such as bare bottom boys, melon eating children, alligators chasing babies, or kids sitting in out houses were always big sellers. Many of these items are still readily available.

In the mid-1950s, when the civil rights movement began, these collectibles began disappearing from the stores. As racial sensitivities grew, they were seen in their derogatory light and were found to be very offensive. Today, however, many of these items are being reproduced in Japan, Korea, England, and Taiwan. The quality is mostly poor, but one needs to do their homework in order not to get fooled by these copies.

Some of the items being reproduced or new items being made are highly collectible. Some of these include the quality cookie jars from Carol Gifford, who lives in Oklahoma, the limited edition Santas from Hallmark cards, and "All God's Children" figurines. Other reproduced items, however, are a lesser quality, an example being the McCoy mammy cookie jar which was reproduced in 1991. As in all things, what you collect is a matter of personal taste. My loves are the smiling mammies and the kitchen items.

In the 1980s the Metlox pottery company came out with a mammy cookie jar with polka dots on her dress. This jar sold for $29 and was a good quality ceramic jar. The company went out of business and now the jar is worth well over $200. One never knows about these things, but don't you wish we had foresight?

This my third published book on black memorabilia. I have tried to show you, the collector, the price the items are demanding on today's market and to give you a description of these collectibles. Only a few of the black memorabilia collectibles shown in these pages were in my previous books. The market will probably demand another book, as there are many more items still waiting to be found. Several other books on these collectibles have been written and they also have many different black memorabilia collectibles. Remember to do your homework on collecting black memorabilia and always know your source! It's always buyer beware in this or any other field of collecting. Happy hunting!

Prices differ in from coast to coast and auction prices differ from shop prices. Prices are also affected by condition and availability.

Kitchen

Salt & Pepper

Chalk mammy salt and pepper set. 4". $65-75.

Ceramic Mammy condiment set. Japan. 7". $65-75.

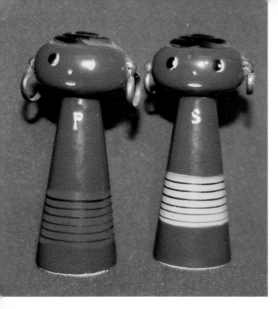

Ceramic native salt and pepper set with brass earrings, 6". Japan. $40-50.

Luzianne mammy salt and pepper set made by the F & F Co. Dayton, Ohio. 5.5" tall. $145-160 pair.

Ceramic mammy and chef, set of salt and peppers. Japan. 4" $65-75.

Ceramic kissing natives, salt and pepper set, 4". Japan. $40-50.

Salt and pepper sets. Ceramic. 3". Japan. $40-50 set.

Ceramic mammy and chef, salt and pepper set. 3". $50-60.

Ceramic mammy and chef, salt and pepper set. Japan. 4.5". $55-65.

Ceramic busts of chef and mammy salt and pepper. 2.5". $85-100 pair.

Ceramic lady and man, salt and pepper set. 2.5". $50-60.

Chalk sitting mammies, salt and pepper set. 2.25". $75-85.

Ceramic mammy and chef busts, salt and pepper set. 3". Japan. $55-65.

Pottery native busts, salt and pepper set. 2". $35-40.

Ceramic "Seven Come Eleven," salt and pepper set on a tray. 2". $50-60.

Wooden chef, salt and pepper set. 5.5". $55-65.

Ceramic clown with seal, salt and pepper set. 4". Japan. $75-85.

Ceramic native heads, salt and pepper set. 5". Japan. $45-55.

Ceramic clown with drum, salt and pepper set. 3.25". Japan. $75-85.

Pottery native on alligator, salt and pepper set. Japan. $45-55.

Ceramic bust of man and watermelon, salt and pepper set. 2.25". $75-85.

Bisque bobbing head woman eating melon, salt and pepper set. 3.5". Made in Japan. $85-100.

Ceramic mammy and chef salt and pepper set. 2.75". Japan. $40-50.

Ceramic young mammy and chef salt and pepper set. 3.5". Japan. $45-55.

Ceramic mammy and chef salt and pepper set. 3.5". $45-55.

Ceramic mammy and chef salt and pepper set. Japan. 4.25" $45-55.

Ceramic mammy and chef salt and pepper set. Japan. 4.5".
$40-50.

Ceramic grease jar with pie bird, and salt and pepper set.
$225-250.

Ceramic grease jar with pie bird, and salt and pepper set. $225-250.

Ceramic grease jar with matching salt and pepper set. $150-175.

Complete ceramic set of "Omnibus" mammy kitchen items. Back row (left to right): tea pot, 8.5". syrup pitcher, 9"; cookie jar, 10". Front row (left to right): butter dish, 7.5" x 5"; salt and pepper, 3"; cream and sugar, 5". $900-1000.

Wall Hangers

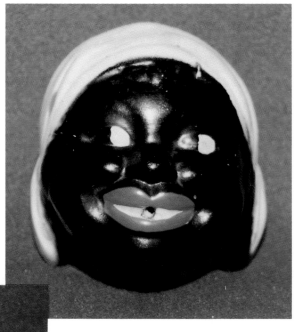

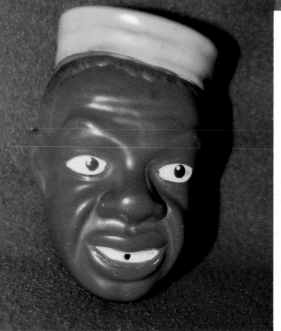

Ceramic mammy string holder. String comes out the mouth. 8". Japan. $450-500.

Pottery porter string holder. 7". String comes out the mouth. $400-450.

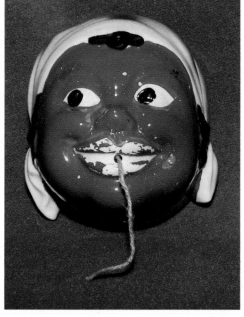

Mammy string holder, 6.5". Japan. Rare. $400-450.

Chalk mammy string holder. String
comes out of her basket. 7". "Marco".
$200-250.

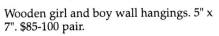

Wooden girl and boy wall hangings. 5" x
7". $85-100 pair.

Plaster chef pot holder hanger. 9.5". $45-
50.

Pressed fiber mammy head with cotton bag for clothes pins.
15.5". $65-75.

Ceramic mammy face wall pocket.
Japan. 5". $175-200.

Hand-made wooden Aunt Jemima
memo and hot pad holder, 9". $40-50.

Hand-made wood mammy pot holder
hanger. 5.25" x 5.5". $40-50.

Wooden hot pad holder. 10". $60-70.

Wooden mammy memo holder. 6.5".
$45-50.

Wooden mammy hot pad holder. 4.5".
$30-35.

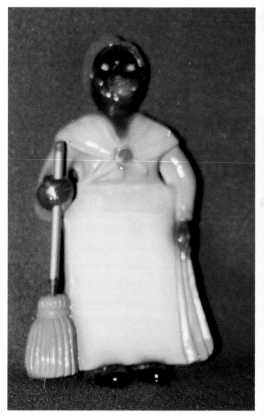

Wooden mammy with 2 babies, hot pad
and note holder.
$70-80.

Chalk mammy memo holder. 10". $65-
70.

Folk art mammy memo holder. 1950s. 10". $30-40.

Pressed fiber mammy note holder. 10". $100-125.

Plastic mammy memo holder. 10". $65-85.

Cardboard mammy memo minder and calendar. 11". $55-65.

Wooden little girl shopping list. 10". $75-85.

Mandy pin cushion. Oil cloth pin holder and cardboard dress. Canada, 8". $50-60.

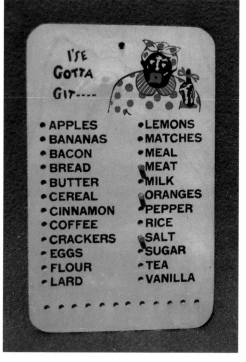

Wooden "I'se Gotta Git" shopping list. 11". $75-85.

APPLES	MEAT
BREAD	MILK
BUTTER	ORANGES
CEREAL	ONIONS
COFFEE	POTATOES
CRACKERS	RICE
EGGS	SALT
EXTRACTS	SPICES
FLOUR	SOAP
LARD	SUGAR
LEMONS	TEA
MATCHES	TOMATOES

Wood mammy memo board. 10". $85-95.

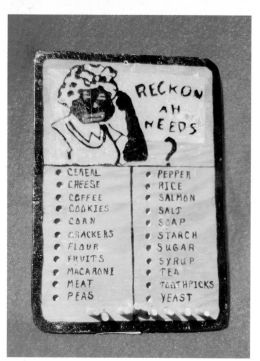

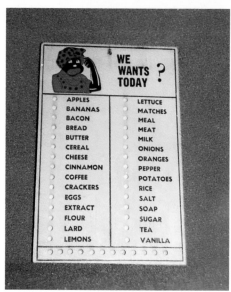

Wood "We wants today" memo board. 9". $80-90.

Hand-made "Reckon ah needs?" grocery board. 8.25" x 6". $60-70.

Wooden shopping list, "Recon ah needs." 8.25". $75-85.

Wooden "I'se can't forget to remember" shopping list. $85-100.

Linens

Cotton "Sunny side up" table cloth. $85-95.

Cotton appliqued and embroidered tea towel. $30-35.

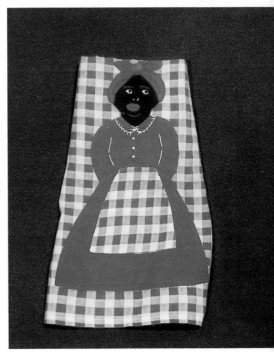

Checkered cotton tea towel with appliqued mammy. $35-40.

Cotton tea towel with embroidered mammy. $30-35.

Embroidered cotton tea towel,"Mah cookin'". $30-35.

Cotton kitchen tea towel with strut-
ting couple. $40-45.

Cotton tea towel with appliqued
chef cutting turkey. $40-45.

Cotton tea towel "To market, to market
to buy a fat pig".
$35-40.

Pair of kitchen tea towels, cotton applique and embroidery. $40-45 each.

Cotton table cloth, square. $150-175.

Cotton tea towel, with embroidered native carrying fruit on his head. $25-30.

Cotton tea towel. Painted mammy making a cake. $40-50.

Kitchen cotton tea towel. Mammy hanging up clothes. $55-65.

Kitchen cotton tea towel. Mammy with basket of fruit. $55-65.

Kitchen cotton tea towel. Mammy
singing in the kitchen.
$50-60.

Kitchen cotton tea towel. Mammy
making pancakes. $60-70.

Cotton kitchen tea towel. $45-55.

Embroidered cotton tea towels. $45-55 each.

Cotton tea towel with applied mammy. $35-40.

Cotton kitchen tea towel. $40-45.

33

Cotton tea towel with appliqued ammy. $40-50.

Silk hand-painted wall hanging. "Martini anyone?" $25-30.

Cotton Aunt Jemima apron. Newer. $20-30.

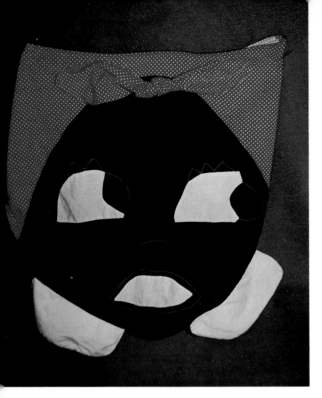

Cotton apron with mammy. $40-45.

Cotton apron with native cooking a man. Barth & Drefuss. $45-55.

Cotton mammy hot pad. 11". $55-65.

Cotton wall hanging hot pad holder. $40-45.

Cotton apron with mammy. $40-45.

Miscellaneous Kitchen Items

Chef, ceramic spoon rest. Japan. 4" x 7".
$85-100.

Ceramic maid soap pad holder. 5" x 5".
$95-110.

Ceramic mammy with curly hair,
scouring pad holder. 5.5" tall. $165-185.

Mammy ceramic soap dish. Germany,
6". $150-185.

"Brownie Downing" saucer. 4". Japan. $45-50.

Ceramic mammy spoon holder. 8". 1977. $15-20.

"Brownie Downing" salt and pepper set. 3.5". Japan. $40-45.

Chalk mammy measuring spoon holder. 5.5". $55-65.

Hand-painted tile with natives dancing. "Brasil." $20-25.

Silver Frederick Douglass spoon. 6".
$450-500.

Sterling spoon with Jonnie Griffin on the
end and "Sunny South" on the handle.
5.5". $150-160.

Sterling spoon with boy's head on the
end. 4". "Brandenton, Fl." in the bowl.
$125-145.

Sterling spoon with "Sunny South"
down the handle and boy's head on the
end. 5". $160-175.

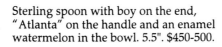

Sterling spoon with boy on the end,
"Atlanta" on the handle and an enamel
watermelon in the bowl. 5.5". $450-500.

Ceramic native with missing egg timer. Japan. 6.5". $125-140.

Ceramic mammy egg timer (egg timer missing). 4". Germany. $110-125.

Bisque chef with egg timer missing. Japan. 3.5". $85-100.

Ceramic (black face) sitting chef holding glass egg timer. Japan. 3". $95-110.

Ceramic (brown face) sitting chef holding glass egg timer. Japan. 3". $95-110.

Ceramic chef holding glass egg timer. 3".
$85-100.

Bisque Golliwog egg timer. "England".
4". $175-200.

Ceramic mammy with spoon and glass
egg timer. 4". Japan. $75-95.

Ceramic chef scouring pad holder. 5".
Occupied Japan.
$185-200.

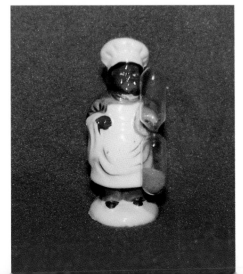

Ceramic chef holding towel and glass
egg timer, 4". Japan.
$85-100.

Ceramic mammy grease jar. Japan. 5.5".
$425-450.

Cotton mammy tissue holder. 11.25".
$20-25.

Ceramic "Brayton Laguna" cookie jar.
13.5". $1100-1400.

Wooden cookie bucket with mammy
painted on front.
7.25" x 8". $65-75.

Ceramic Rio Rita cookie jar from
"Fritz and Floyd." 12".
$150-200.

Ceramic Santa tea pot. "Oci Taiwan." 9.5". $175-200.

Ceramic Mrs. Santa cookie jar. "Oci Taiwan." 9.5". $175-200.

12 oz. hand-painted minstrel frosted glasses. $30-40 each.

Ceramic mug. 4.75". $40-45.

1957 drinking glass from the Milwaukee Braves. $15-20.

Ceramic drinking cup from Italy. Boy eating melon on front. 4". $95-110.

Drinking glass with native dancing around an elephant. 12 oz. $20-25.

Ceramic chef spoon rest. 4.25". Japan. $65-75.

Ceramic mammy creamer. Japan. 4.5". $100-125.

Tankard with banjo man of front. "Bavaria". 6". $500-550.

China creamer and cup set. 2.5". $85-100 set.

Mississippi souvenir wooden hamburger maker. Japan. 5.5". $30-40.

Ceramic mammy spoon rest. 3" x 6.5". $60-70.

Round "Ole Vir-Gin-a" ginger bread pan. $40-45.

Ole Vir-Gin-A ginger bread pan. 4.5" x 9". $40-45.

Oblong "Ole Vir-Gin-A" gingerbread pan. 9". $40-45.

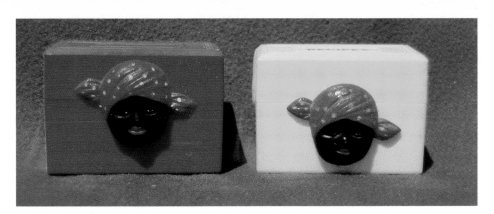

F & F plastic recipe boxes. They came in red, yellow and green. $250-275.

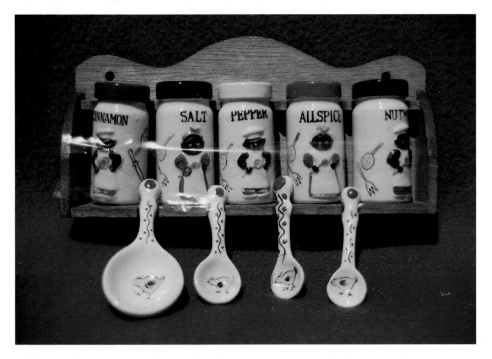

Ceramic spice set in wooden rack with measuring spoons. Each spice 3". $140-160.

Bisque bobbing head match holder. Japan, 3". $75-100.

Ceramic pie bird with Golliwogs on front. England. $85-100.

"Room Service" dinner plate by Doug Wilson. 10". $65-75.

Ceramic mammy bell, plaid. 3.5". $65-75.

Man sugar container. Made in England, Kentington. 11". $155-180.

Restaurant

Restaurant Items

Pin back button from Mammy's Shanty in Atlanta, Georgia. $15-18.

Match book with mammy on cover. $7-9.

Matches from Golden West Hotel, San Diego, California.
$15-18.

Matches from Pickaninny Coffee Shop. $8-10.

Matches from Mammy's Shanty, Atlanta, Georgia. $10-12.

Matches from Pick-A-Rib restaurant. $12-15.

"Cream of Wheat" cereal bowl with Spirit of Saint Louis inside. 6.5". Made in U.S.A. $125-150.

Cardboard sample box of "Cream of Wheat." 3.5". $85-100.

Paper towel, "Yas'suh! dis am a towel!" $20-30.

Match book from Reebs in Columbus, Ohio. $8-10.

Wooden Sambo's restaurant free coffee tokens. $4-5 each.

Cardboard menu from Sambo's restaurant. 9.25". $85-100.

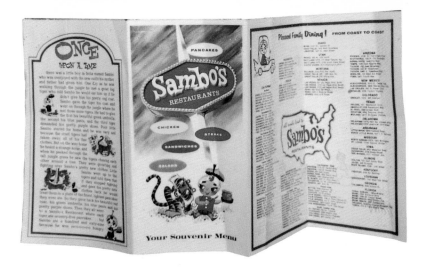

Paper "Sambo Restaurant" menu. $85-100.

Cardboard Sambo chocolate drink carrier. $65-75.

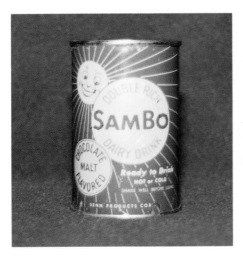

Tin can of Sambo chocolate drink. $75-85.

Ceramic Sambo's restaurant cup. 8 oz. "U.S.A". $35-40.

Three different Sambo's restaurant match books. $10-15 each.

Aunt Jemima ceramic cream pitcher. 3.5". $40-50.

Sample package of "Aunt Jemima" waffles. $20-25.

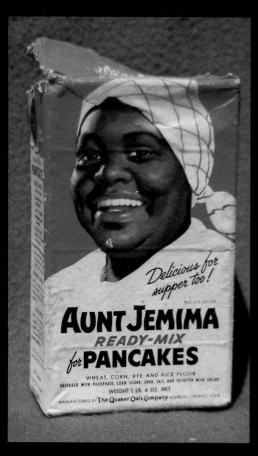

Box of Aunt Jemima Ready Mix for Pancakes. $85-100.

Aunt Jemima Yellow Corn Meal bag. 25 lbs. $165-185.

Paper souvenir hat from Aunt Jemima promotional breakfasts. $50-60.

Coon Chicken Inn match book. $15-20.

Cardboard menu from Cotton Patch
restaurant. 14". San Diego, California.
$70-80.

Menu from Dinah's restaurant, Palo Alto. $65-85

Advertising

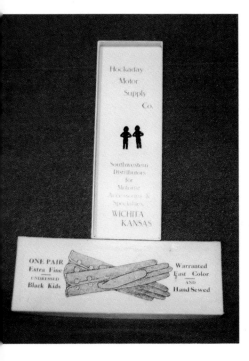

Black kid gloves box with two china black babies inside. 1920. $125-150.

Magazine ad for "Colored Kids" gloves. $25-30.

Green River Whiskey, rubber advertising piece. $175-190.

Colgate Weekend Package in cardboard box. 5" x 3". $35-40.

Cardboard Gold Dust sign. 12" x 22".
$500-550.

Box of "Sharpoint" cobbler's nails. 1.75".
$60-75.

Fatou and Soriba wooden matches. 1.5"
x 2". $30-40.

"John" cigar box, ca. 1887. $140-160.

Package of Dar'Kie Peppermints. New
$10-12.

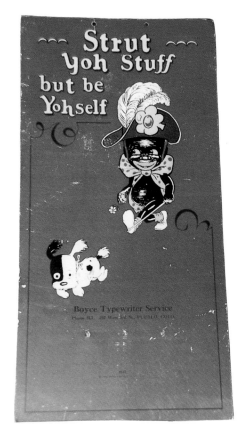

Cotton Club match book. $8-10

Cardboard advertising for "Boyce
typewriters, Pueblo, Co." 1926. 13" x 7".
1926. $65-80.

Cotton "Dixie Kid Cut Plug Tobacco" bag. Louisville, Kentucky. 5." $150-175.

Cantelope smoking tobacco, 1883. Kansas City, Missouri. 6.75". $450-500.

Bottle of herbs and seasonings of New Orleans. 3". $45-55.

Mammy's Orange Soda. 64 oz. Philadelphia, Pennsylvania. $125-150.

Just Rite electric barbecue pot. Chef on the front. "Southern Style Foods Co. Nashville, Tenn." $225-250.

Log cabin wooden cigar box. 9" x 6". $450-500.

Wooden orange crate with porter on label. $75-90.

Pencil holder advertising "Oxydol Soap Powder." Walker Co. St. Louis, Missouri. $75-85.

Black Magic Humus. Two dry quarts. $20-25.

Black Magic Charcoal for gardening. 9 oz. $20-25.

Glass African, figural bottle of Trinidad "Old Oak Rum". 11" $30-40.

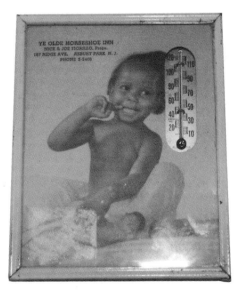

Thermometer advertising picture. Asbury Park, New Jersey. 4" x 5". $30-40.

Tins

Luzianne sample coffee tin. 3". "Reily & Co." $175-200.

Tin for Warrenton Rum Cakes by Mary Clement. 7". $40-50.

Dinah Black Enamel paint tin. Quarter pint. $80-95.

Dinah Black Enamel tin, quart. Chicago, Montreal, Los Angeles, Boston. $125-145.

Luzianne 12 oz. coffee tin. Reily Co. $45-50.

Duncan's Admiration Coffee tin. 5.5",
1932, Texas. $145-160.

Bixby's "Satinola" shoe polish tin. New
York, 2.25". $55-65.

Advertising cardboard tin. "Dr.
LeGear's Lice Powder." St. Louis,
Missouri. 2.5". $65-75.

"Mascot Baking Powder" tin. The
bakers are carrying a pyramid of bread.
4". $85-100.

Mason's Shoe Polish tin. "Mine Mf'g. Co." $45-55.

"Sunny South" peanut tin. 3.5" x 8". $140-150.

Advertising tin for "Excelsior Varnish Works - Turpentine Black Asphaltum." 4.5". $145-165.

Horn clear varnish tin. Long Island, New York. $35-40.

8" Ideal Blend Coffee tin. Jones and Co., New York. $125-150.

Dickey's White Side Wall Tire Cleaner tin. 4". St. Louis. $85-100.

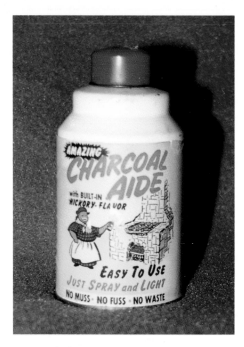

Can of Charcoal Aide. Mammy spraying her outdoor grill. 5.5". "Chicago, Empire Oil Co." 11 oz. $65-80.

Tin of Tom's Hostess peanuts with butler. 3". $60-70.

Advertising tin "Negri Vert Groen". Chrome cleaner. 4.25". $65-70.

Tin can of Ole Virginny cashews with mammy. 4.5". $60-75.

Southern plantation tin, "Home on the Mississippi." $40-50.

Ephemera

Cards & Post Cards

Greeting card. "Po' li'l me." $7-8.

Greeting card, "To you at Thanksgiving." $6-7.

Paper greeting card. "Happy birthday to you." $6-7.

Paper greeting card. $7-8.

Paper greeting card. "Happy birthday."
$8-10.

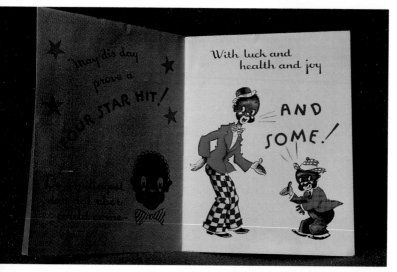

Paper greeting card. "To a shut in." $8-10.

Valentine, "But ah sighs fo' you". $5-60.

Advertising card for "Ayer's Cathartic Pills." $15-20.

Mammy Christmas card. $6-70.

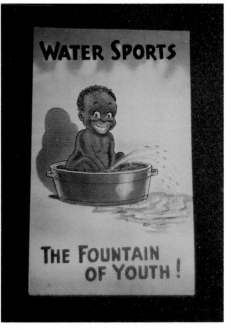

Post card, "Water sports". $8-10.

Post card, "Help, help". 1908. $15-18.

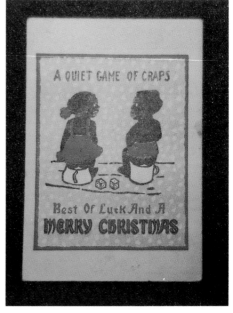

Post card, "A quiet game of craps". $10-12.

Post card, "A study in black and white". $12-15.

Post card, "Pushin a good thing along". $7-8.

"Mammy to me, come an help," 1907. $12-15.

Post card with porter and trip ticket in envelope. $15-18.

Post card, "Thanksgiving, lost by a tail". $10-12.

Post card, "I'm in a dreadful hurry". $8-10.

Post card, "I am sending you a pair of black kids". $10-12.

Post card, "Paging Mr.—." $8-10.

Post card, "Help, you'd holler too!" $6-7.

Post card, "Don't you fool me chile no mo'." $6-7.

Golliwog cardboard card. Raphael Tuck & Sons. 8" x 8". $60-75.

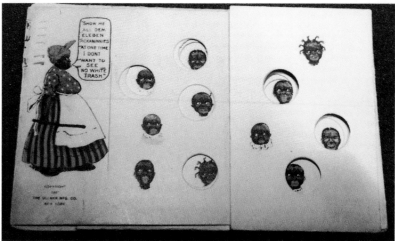

"Pick the Pickaninnies" puzzle, post card. You must turn the pages until all black babies show, "no white trash allowed". $65-75.

"Cupid Awake" and "Cupid Asleep" in original tin frames. 4" x 5". $200-250 set.

Paper mammy mask.
9" X 7." $150-165.

Opposite page bottom:
Set of children dancing, drawings by
Janice May. 8" x 10". $85-95.

5" x 7" photo of black football team. 1920s. $35-40.

8" x 12" photo of black nuns. 1929. $40-50.

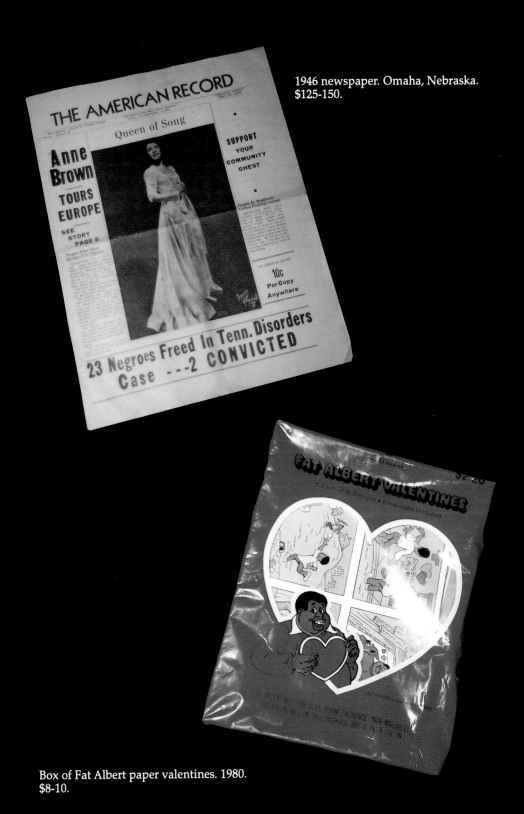

1946 newspaper. Omaha, Nebraska.
$125-150.

Box of Fat Albert paper valentines. 1980.
$8-10.

Books

Little Black Sambo story book. Rand-McNally, 1959. $75-85.

Little Black Sambo book. Hardback. 1942. 13" x 10." $85-100.

Little Black Sambo story book, 1927. $125-150.

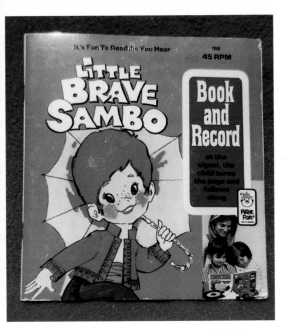

Little Brave Sambo book and record with a white Sambo. 1971 by Ambassador Records. $30-40.

Miniature *Little Black Sambo* story book. Platte-Monk, 1927.$135-150.

Miniature *Little Black Sambo* book. $80-100.

Little Black Sambo book. "Linenette." Sam'l Gabriel & Son, 1921. $85-100.

Little Black Sambo "Golden Book," 1946.
$100-125.

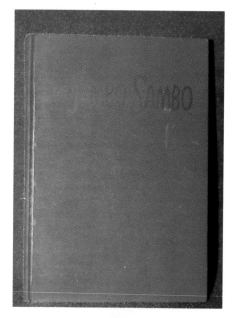

This *Jumbo Sambo* book has all Helen Bannerman's stories. 1937. $55-65.

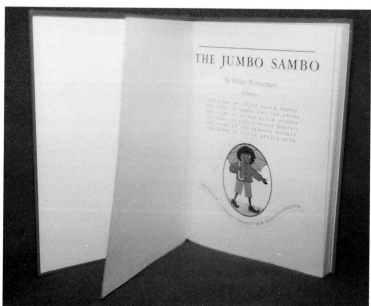

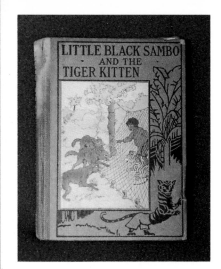

Little Black Sambo and the Tiger Kitten book, 1926, by Howard Altemus. $120-145.

Story of Little Black Sambo by Whitman Pub. Co., 1937. $85-100.

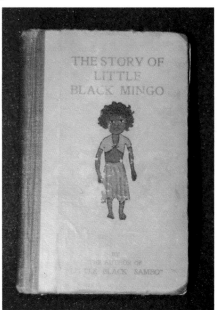

The Story of Little Black Mingo. $85-100.

Little Black Sambo story book, 1959. Whitman. $85-100.

Wooden scrap book, mammy on front. 8" x 12". $20-25.

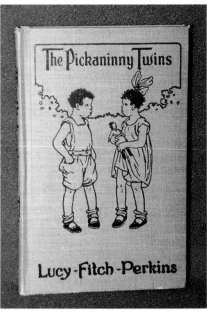

The Pickaninny Twins. Lucy-Fitch-Perkins, 1931. $75-85.

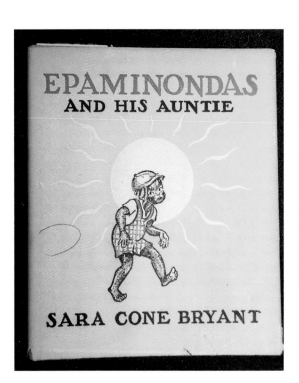

Epaminondas and His Auntie. Sara Cone Bryant, 1938. $65-75.

Epaminondas Helps in the Garden by Constance Egan, 1959. $60-70.

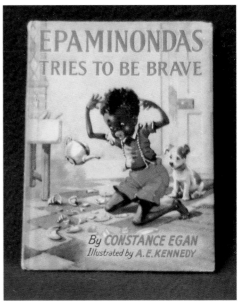

My Dollies Story Book, "Linentex" book by Saalfield Pub. Co., 1921. $60-70.

Epaminondas Tries to be Brave by Constance Anderson, 1960. $60-70.

Paper back, *Ten Little Niggers* by Agatha Christie, 1963. $15-20.

Travel Friends, "Linenette" story book by Sam Gabriel and Sons, 1940. $55-65.

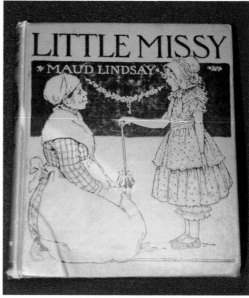

Story book Little Missy by Maud Lindsay. 1922. $60-70.

Story book, Watermelon Pete by Elizabeth Gordon, 1938. $50-60.

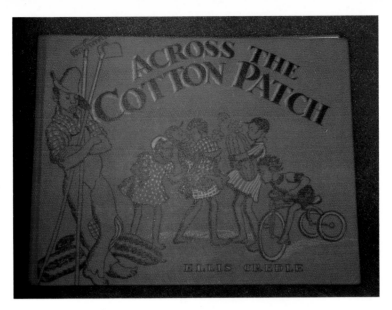

Across the Cotton Patch, story book. 1935. $55-65.

Story book, *The Cocoa Dancer* illustrated
by Gladys Blackwood, 1945. $55-65.

Beloved Belindy story book, 1926.
P.F. Volland. $160-180.

Story book, *All Kinds of Kids* by R.H. Carman, 1907. $40-50.

Petunia be Keerful by Anne Christopher, 1934. $65-75.

The Children's Uncle Tom's Cabin story book. 1938. $65-75.

Story book of *Black Alice*, 1968. Thom Demijohn. $30-40.

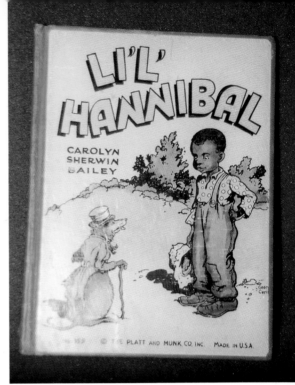

Li'l' Hannibal by Carolyn Bailey, 1938. $55-65.

Topsy Turvy's Pigtails by Bernice Anderson, 1935. $50-60.

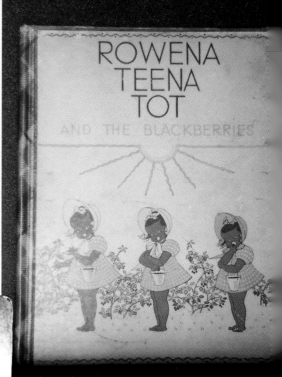

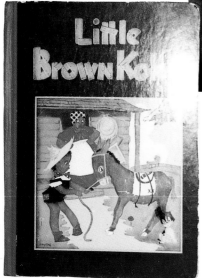

Roweena, Teena, Tot and the Blackberries, story book by Fannie Bloomberg, 1934. $75-85.

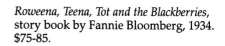

Little Brown Koko story book by American Colortype Co. 1951. $75-85.

Amelia Jane Again! by Enid Blyton." $60-75.

The Strange Tale of Ten Little Nigger Boys
by the Pilgrims.
$85-100.

I'se Topsy! Child's story book by Raphael
Tuck, 1902. $125-150.

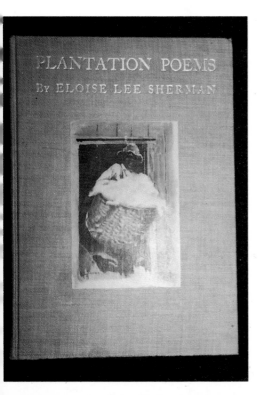

Plantation Poems. Eloise Sherman, 1910.
$125-150.

Kentucky Fare paperback recipe book, by Margaret Bridwell. 1953. $30-40.

"Doughboy Joe" minstrel play by J. Hal Connor. Eldridge Entertainment House, 1929. $15-20.

"Funny Jokes and Stories," 1920. $50-60.

Booklet on "The Black Face Joker," 1918. $70-80.

Paperback Black-Face Fun & Minstrel Guide. 1925. $45-50.

Book on *Louisiana Voodoo* by Andre Cajun, 1946. $20-25.

Sheet Music
& Records

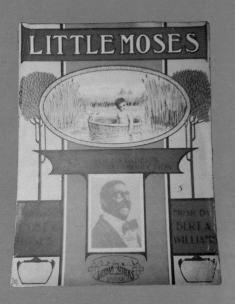

Sheet music. "Short'nin Bread," John W. Schaum. $40-45.

Sheet music, "Little Moses" by Lew Dockstader. $30-40.

1918 sheet music. "When You Sang Hush-A-Bye to Me," by Fedria Logan. $40-50.

Sheet music, "Swing along" by Jacques Wolfe. $30-35.

Sheet music. "I Never Had a Mammy," by "Topsy and Eva." $40-45.

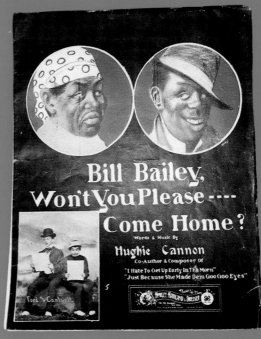

Sheet music. "Bill Bailey, Won't You Please Come Home?" 1902. Hughie Cannon, $30-40.

Trade card for Union Pacific Trade Co., "I'm daddy's baby." $35-40.

Sheet music. "Ma Rainbow Coon," Greene & Sloane, 1910. $40-50.

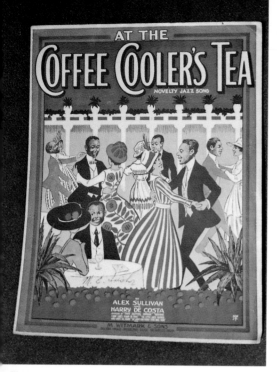

Sheet music. "At the Coffee Cooler's Tea," Sullivan & De Costa, 1918. $30-40.

Sheet music. "I Don't Care if Yo' Nebber Comes Back," Brown & Rosenfeld, 1897. $40-50.

Sheet music. "Bees-Wax Rag," Harry J. Lincoln, 1909. $35-45.

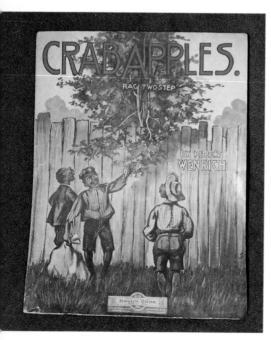

Sheet music. "Crab Apples," Percy Weinrich, 1898. $25-30.

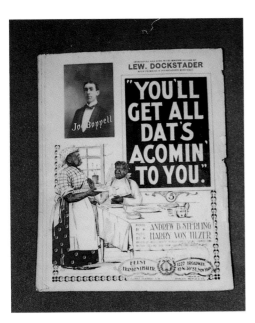

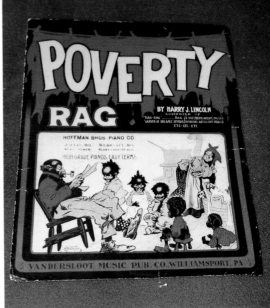

Sheet music. "Poverty Rag," Harry J. Lincoln, 1909. $45-55.

Sheet music. "You'll Get All Dat's Acomin' to You," Sterling and Von Tilzer, 1898. $45-55.

Sheet music. "Jig Walk," "Jo" Trent and Duke Ellington, 1924. $40-50.

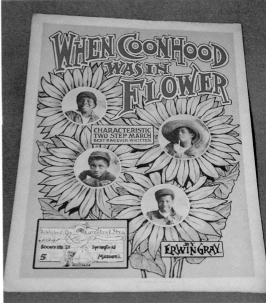

Sheet music. "When Coonhood Was in Flower," Erwin Gray, 1901. $50-60.

Sheet music. "I Don't Know
Where I'm Goin but I'm on
My Way," John Bren,
1905. $35-40.

Front and back of plastic record.
"Blue Tail Fly" and "Carry Me
Back to Old Virginny."
$75-80.

Cardboard picture record. "Gilt Edge,
Cecil Boogie". 10".
$70-85.

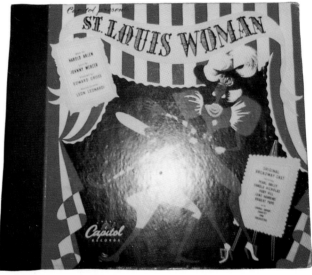

"Saint Louis Woman"
record album. $70-80.

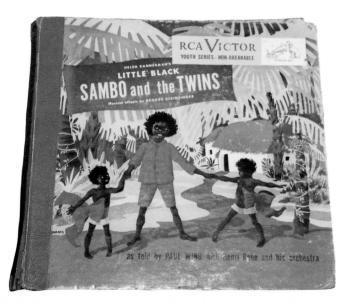

"Sambo and the Twins"
record album. $60-70.

And More...

Figurines & Wall Plaques

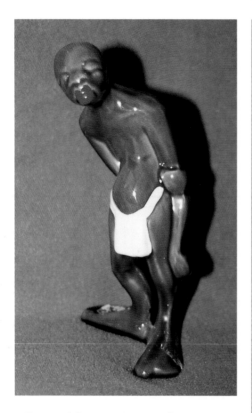

Pottery African native man figurine.
10.25". $30-35.

Pottery African native woman figurine.
8.25". $35-45.

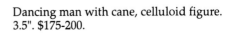

Dancing man with cane, celluloid figure.
3.5". $175-200.

Ceramic figurine, girl in raincoat, 5.5".
$45-50.

Wooden hand-carved mammy figurine.
4.5". $60-75.

Copper shoeshine boy statue on marble
base. Circa 1850. 9.5". $450-500.

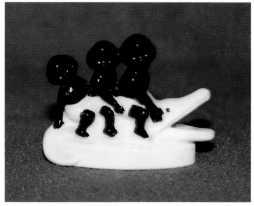

China figure of three boys sitting on
alligator. Japan. 2.5" x 3.5". $85-100.

Pot metal banjo player ash tray. Hat lifts
up for the ash tray. Circa 1880s. $500-
600.

Pair of ceramic African dancers, wall
figurines. 8". $45-60.

Pair of carved wood busts of natives. 8". $165-190.

Venetian glass black clown holding glass ball. 6". $95-120.

Pot metal man sitting on cotton basket made of cast iron.
7.25" x 5". $600-700.

Wooden bobbing head native carrying a baby on her back. 6". $35-40.

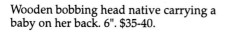

Topsy felt figurine. Brazil. 4". $20-25.

Ceramic native figurines. 3.75". $40-45.

Bisque musician figurines, set of 5. 2". $150-175.

Ceramic blond hair native figurine. 6".
"Catalina." $35-40.

Wooden native figurine, 6". $15-20.

Ceramic blackamoor figurines. Japan.
8.5". $45-55 pair.

Ceramic hors d'oeuvres butler , holds
tooth picks. 8". $50-60.

Carved wooden figurines of musicians.
5.5". $60-75 pair.

Cast iron door stop. Man on bale of cotton. 9.5" x 7.5". $450-500.

Glass African musician, figural bottle of "Drioll cream de menthe". 12". $50-60.

Plaster African dancer bust bookends. 7" x 8". $30-40.

Ceramic native figurine. 3.5". $40-45.

Wrought iron bike and man with
wooden head figurine. 9.5". $40-50.

Ceramic native lady figurine. 3.5". $40-
45.

Singing woman perfume bottle. Italy.
$165-185.

Banjo player and dancing man on Japan planter. Ceramic, 2.75". $40-45.

Blackamoor figurine. Pot metal, 5". $200- 225.

Blackamoor ceramic vase. Occupied Japan. 5.5". $20-25.

Majolica vase with lady holding flowers. 11.5". $425-450

Ceramic planter, man playing mandolin.
$40-50.

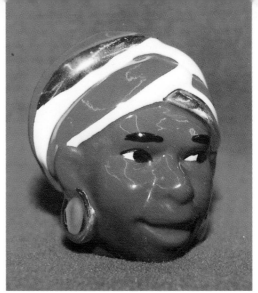

Native ceramic planter, marked
"Brayton Laguna". 3.5".
$70-80.

Native ceramic planter, 4". $50-60.

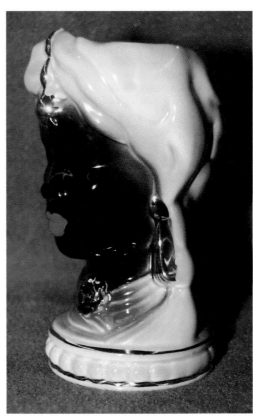

Blackamoor lady's head planter.
"Shawnee," 7.5". $80-100.

Plaster African figurines. "Coventry Ware". 10". $45-50 pair.

Aluminum minstrel man wall plaque.
5.5". $65-75

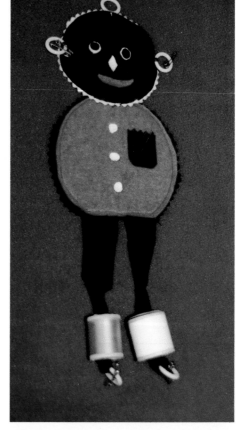

Native sewing kit and thread holder
made from felt, 12". $25-30.

Jewelry

Cast iron miniature mammy charm. $15-20.

Sterling blackamoor pin. 3.25". $75-85.

Native mask silver earrings. 2.75". $65-75.

Green river advertising watch fob. 4.75". $85-100.

Yarn golliwog pin. 2.5". $45-55.

Ceramic pin. Bust of lady wearing lace and button hat. 4".
$75-85.

Wood man's face pin with straw hat. 2.75". $55-65.

Ivory and brass pin with bust of native and brass crossed weapons. 1.5". $275-300.

Banjo playing man pin, made of pot metal. Moveable eyes. 3". $55-65.

Wooden sailor boys pin. 3". $50-60.

Ceramic and plastic blackamoor pin. 3". $150-165.

Molded ceramic 3.25" pin and 1.5" earrings, with copper headband and earrings on natives. $160-180.

Ceramic man pin. 3". $100-115.

Plaster native lady with hat, pin. 2". $80-100.

Bakelite base with ceramic lady's head pin. 2.25". $80-100.

Teakwood native man's head pin with glass colored stones in eyes, ears, neck and hair. 3.25". $140-160.

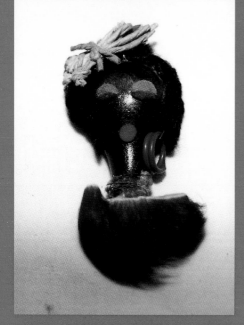

Wood and fur native lady's head pin. 3.5". $75-100.

Native lady wood pin with exaggerated lips. 3". $150-175.

Native man with bone earrings, carved wood pin. 3". $140-160.

Native man carved wood pin with copper necklace and glass eyes. 4.5". $140-160.

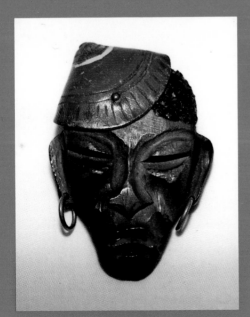

Afro lady pin, carved wood with copper earrings. 3.5". $145-170.

Native wood pin with brass ring in nose and brass head trim. 3". $135-150.

Carved wood pin with Bakelite hair. 3.5". $175-195.

Carved wood bust pin of native woman with exaggerated features. Rope on hair and neck pieces, beads in ears. 4.25". $125-145.

Ceramic lady's painted face pin with straw hat. 3". $140-165.

Afro man's head pin set in a Bakelite form. 3". $145-165.

Wood little girl pin with yarn hair and wood fruit bowl hat. 2". $95-125.

Ceramic native woman's head pin with straw hat and bakelite head decoration. 3". $115-135.

Wood native man's head pin. Brass earrings and neck piece. 3.5". $125-140.

Ceramic lady's head pin with ceramic fruit on head. 3.25". $85-100.

Teakwood Afro woman's pin with stone set in cheek. 3.5". $160-185.

African mask ceramic pin with rope hair. 4.25". $125-140.

Wooden banjo playing man pin. 4". Hand-painted. $145-160.

Brass native mask pin with glass stones for decoration. 2.75". $135-150.

Plastic native pin with moveable eyes. 3". $85-100.

Wooden native pin with yarn hair and moveable eyes. 3". $70-80.

Native figures on bracelet. Pot metal and Bakelite. 1" charms. $115-145.

Blackamoor with harp, pot metal and rhinestone pin. "Coro." 2.25". $125-150.

Blackamoor copper pendant. 2.5". $45-55.

Copper native mask pendant. 2.5". $55-65.

Plastic blackamoor clip-on earrings.
1.25". $60-70.

Blackamoor pin. Brass and pot metal.
2.25". $60-85.

Blackamoor Bakelite bracelet. 6.5".
$125-150.

Blackamoor, Bakelite
bracelet, earrings and
necklace. $150-175 set.

Blackamoor pin and earrings set. Sterling and onyx. $85-100.

Pot metal and rhinestone blackamoor pin. 3.25". $150-175.

Blackamoor pins and earrings. Pot metal with rhinestone trim. 2" pins. $100-125 set.

Jeweled pencil with blackamoor head on end. 4". $55-65.

Smoking Items

Tin match holder and striker. 3" X 4".
Little girl on front.
$85-100.

Wooden folk art ashtray. Holes for
matches in the hat. 5".
$40-50.

Blackamoor metal head match box. 2".
$125-140.

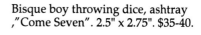

Bisque ashtray, "Come Seven." 2.5" x
2.75". Japan. $40-50.

Bisque boy throwing dice, ashtray
,"Come Seven". 2.5" x 2.75". $35-40.

Naughty nude boy in tub. "He pee's in the water." Porcelain, Japan. $180-200.

Ceramic ash tray with decal of musician in center. Italy. 13". $45-55.

Black Indian ashtray. Japan. 3.5" x 4". $35-40.

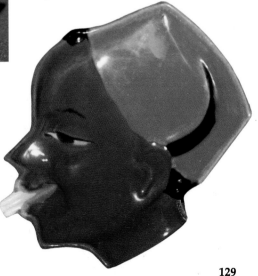

Servant, ceramic ashtray. 6". $45-50.

Ceramic native with tongue wagging ash tray. "Patent TT". 3.75" x 2.5". $65-85.

Majolica cigarette and match holder. Austria. 7.5". $500-525.

Pottery cigarette holder. Man with shoe shine boy. "959".
8" x 7". $165-190.

Majolica humidor, 7". Hat lifts off to insert tobacco. $550-600.

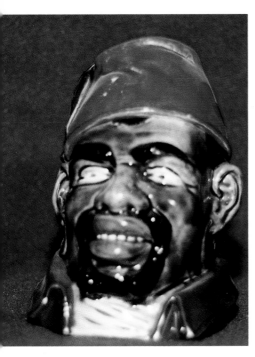

Majolica humidor, 8". Hat lifts off. $450-500.

Pottery humidor. Bandanna lifts off. Hand-painted, 8". $600-650.

Majolica humidor, 7". Hair lifts off. $475-500.

Pottery humidor with boy coming out the side of a bale of cotton. 5". $600-700.

131

Pottery man's head humidor. "#8466 C.K. Linet." 5". $450-500.

Wooden pencil holder of boy pulling donkey. 2.5". $35-45.

Mammy cork for bottle. 2". $15-20.

Tin cigarette holder with tin figures of men and umbrellas sitting on top. 2.25". $300-350.

Aluminum naughty nude lady bottle opener. 12". Japan. $125-150.

Glass drink mixers, 4.5". Painted heads of black man. $7-8.

"Southern Comfort" mixer. Black man serving a white man. $175-200.

Set of four cork coasters. $20-30.

Tin serving snack tray. Jazz band painted on front. $20-30.

Wood cork screw bottle opener. 5". $25-30.

Wooden serving tray. Decals of bell boys on front. 17" x 13". $100-125.

Dolls

Composition boy doll. "Bye Bye Baby," Seiberling Latex Co., U.S.A. 8.5". $150-175.

Hand puppet, cloth body, pressed fiber head. 7". $135-150.

Composition topsy-turvy doll with cloth body. White on one side black on the other. 12". $175-200.

Cotton-stuffed topsy-turvy rag doll. 9".
$40-50.

Topsy-turvy doll with cotton stuffing
and body. 13". $40-50.

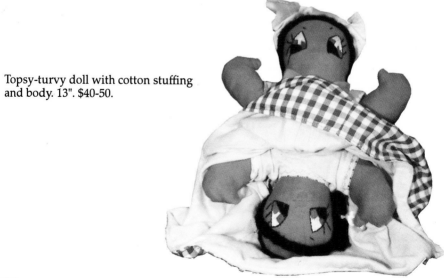

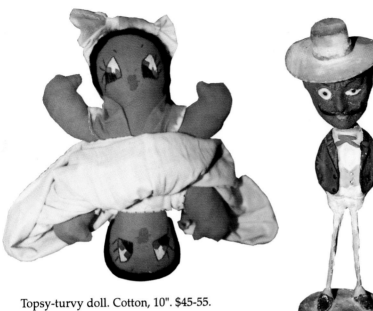

Topsy-turvy doll. Cotton, 10". $45-55.

Primitive crepe paper doll. Pull the string and her arms and legs move. 14.5". $30-40.

Papier maché bobber head figure. 8". $125-140.

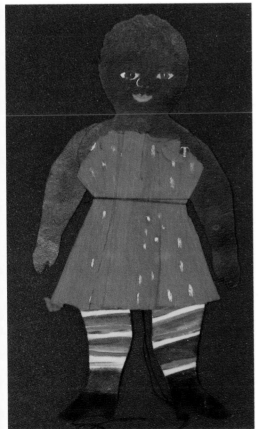

Chef doll hand puppet, with composition head, cloth arms, and cotton dress over a spring body. 6". $250-300. Rare.

Nipple baby doll. 3.25". $20-25.

Nipple doll with baby. 3.5". $25-30.

Crochet mammy doll. 4.5". $15-20.

All cotton mammy finger doll with white babies in her arms. "Souvenir of New Orleans". 4". $50-60.

Celluloid doll on silk melon, pin cushion. 2.5". $75-80.

Cloth rag doll, cotton-stuffed. 15.5". $60-75.

Cotton-stuffed mammy. "Is'e your honey girl." Art Fabric Mills, New York. 5". $160-175.

Home made cloth dolls with rubber heads. 13". $40-50 each.

Cotton-stuffed rag doll, girl with melon, 7". $125-140.

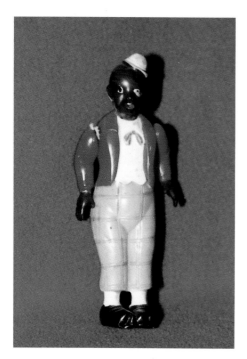

Plastic jointed African doll. 4.5". $25-30.

Celluloid jointed-arms minstrel doll, with painted suit. Japan. 6.5". $85-100

Rubber boy doll. 10". $15-20.

Papier maché jointed lady holding baby. 12". $350-400.

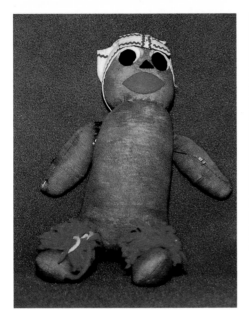

Hand-made 6" doll, cloth body with cotton stuffing. 1940s. $65-75.

Rag doll, cotton-stuffed. 14". $65-75.

Cotton-stuffed boy and girl rag dolls. 17". $60-70 pair.

Papier maché jointed minstrel doll. 12.5" $350-400.

Stuffed soft cotton sock doll. 16". $75-85.

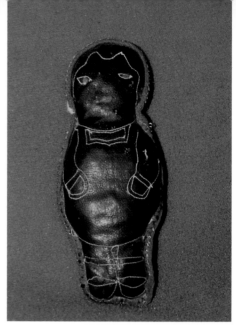

Hard packed, cotton-filled, oil cloth doll. 8". $45-50.

Minstrel doll with papier maché head and cloth body. Stuffed with straw, 10.5". $550-600.

Early stuffed rag doll, cotton, 12". $80-100.

Amos wooden jointed doll. "Hall & Co." 6". $300-350

Inflatable plastic little girl doll. 20". 1990. $20-30.

Cotton-stuffed rag doll. 18". $125-150.

Wooden spool doll. 4". $10-12.

Rubber mammy doll's head. 3.5". $100-125.

Jointed wooden "Andy" toy on a string. 6". $300-350.

Chalk baby native bank (newer). 7". $25-30.

Felt minstrel doll with cotton stuffing. 11". Japan. $60-75.

Topsy-turvy doll, cotton-stuffed with
silk dress. $85-100.

Toys

Cardboard block with a Golliwog. 1.5".
$8-10.

Three wood blocks, Beloved Belindy,
Raggedy Ann and Andy. 1.5". $6-7 each.

Old Maid playing cards
with Melon Moe and Lily
White cards. $30-40.

Old Maid playing cards with
Honey Pie and Seedy Sambo
cards. $40-50.

Deck of playing cards with cotton
pickers on front. $65-75.

Old Maid playing cards with black Sambo. $45-55.

Deck of game cards with black man called Schwarz Peter. Germany. $75-85.

"Shufflin along" playing cards in the box. $125-150.

Bakelite baby toy. 5". $125-150.

Half coconut face string holder. $30-40.

Papier maché boy with melon. Squeeze the melon and he opens his mouth. 4.5". $185-200.

Plastic roly poly toy. 4". $60-65.

Wooden pull toy. "Hustler Toy Co," 11". $195-225.

148

Jester figure with lead ball inside to make it tumble. 3.5". $125-150.

Papier maché mammy roly poly. 5.5". $275-300.

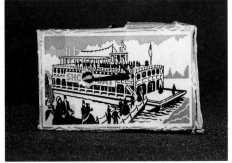

Cardboard show boat movie. Crank the handle on the side and the reel goes around flipping the scenes. "Anchor Mf'g. Co., Springfield, Mo." 3" x 4". $50-60.

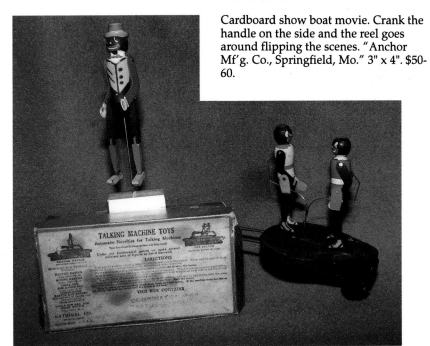

Talking machine toy. The figures move as the record turns; the man dances and the boxers box. 1918. $250-275.

Child's tin plate with boy painted inside. 4.25". Child's tin cup with girl and boy painted on side. 2.5". $250-275 set.

Clown hitting golliwog with hammer, tin toy. Pincher on back side. 4". $150-175.

Tin clacker with bright color minstrel on front. 4". $65-75.

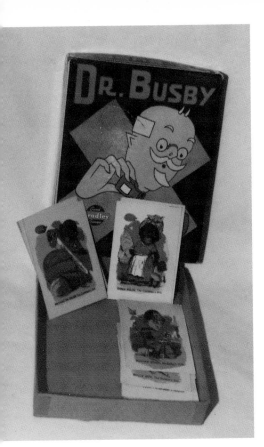

"Dr. Busby" game by Milton Bradley, Springfield, Mass. $25-35.

"African Golf" one cent game," 17" x 18". Tin with wood base. Insert a penny and metal balls fall into the slot. Push down the knob to release and snap balls into dice slots. $900-1100.

"Our Gang" paper dolls. No clothes. $50-75 as is.

"Alabama Coon" cardboard game. Spears Games, designed in England. $250-300.

Miscellaneous

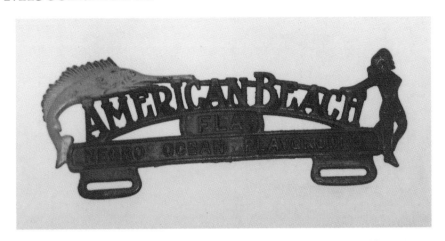

Brass sign from "American Beach, Fla: Negro Ocean Playground." $300-350.

9" flue cover. Rare. Cardboard inserted into tin cover. $225-250.

Wind up "Lux" clock. Topsy eating melon. 3" x 4". $200-225.

Golliwog tin by "Reiley and Co., England." 3.75" x 5.5". $90-100.

Ceramic powder box with butler on the lid. Japan. 3" x 5". $200-250.

Wax Christmas choir boy candle. 3.5".
$25-30.

Pot metal minstrel man pencil sharpener. Germany. 2".
$200-225.

Plastic minstrel pencil sharpener. 2.5".
$150-175.

Pot metal pencil sharpener. The lips are
the blade. Germany. 1.5". $175-200.

Teakwood ink well with glass insert. Native heads are on the sides with their lips
holding the pen. 9" x 5". $80-100.

"Halloween Hattie." Mammy with lollipop head, holding baby. "C. Rosen Co," 8.5". $40-50.

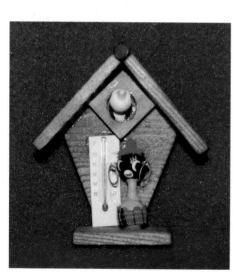

Native wall thermometer. Japan. Wood, 4". $20-25.

Wooden clothes brush mammy with plastic bristles. 4.5". $45-50.

Porter, wooden clothes brush with straw bristles. 8". $75-90.

Hand-made, pressed wood girl and boy
yard ornaments. 18". $50-60 pair.

Quilted doll quilt with printed Aunt
Jemimas. $85-95.

Mardi Gras costume. Papier maché head with cotton dress. Life-size figure. $500-600.

Rare beaded mesh bag with Josephine
Baker on front. Beaded in light blue
beads. 5" x 7". $700-800.

Brass tobacco leaf with boy wearing a
hat coming out the leaf. 21" tall, 10"
wide. Extremely rare. No markings.
$3000-4000.

Bibliography

Carson, Jeanette. *Black Ethnic Collectible Magazine*, Hyattsville, Maryland.

Congdon-Martin, Douglas. *Images in Black: 150 Years of Black Collectibles*. West Chester, Pennsylvania: Schiffer Publishing Ltd. 1990.

Lindenberger, Jan. *Black Memorabilia in the Kitchen*. Atglen, Pennsylvania: Schiffer Publishing, Ltd., 1992.

_____. *Black Memorabilia Around the House*. Atglen, Pennsylvania: Schiffer Publishing, Ltd., 1993.

Morgan, Hal. *Symbols in America*. New York: Viking Penguin Inc. 1986.

Rainwater, Dorothy. *American Spoons: Souvenir & Historical*. Atglen, Pennsylvania: Schiffer Publishing, Ltd., 1990.

Reno, Dawn. *Collecting Black Americana*. New York: Crown Publishers Inc., 1986,

Smith, Darrell A. *Black Americana: A Personal Collection*. Minneapolis, Minnesota: Star Press, Inc., 1988.

Young, Jackie. *Black Collectibles: Mammy and Her Friends*. West Chester, Pennsylvania: Schiffer Publishing, 1988.

World Book Encyclopedia, 1991.